Beer is good for you

A comical collection of quotes for beer lovers

Copyright © Bell & Mackenzie Publishing Limited 2017
First published in the United Kingdom in 2017 by Bell & Mackenzie
Publishing Limited.

All rights reserved. This book or any portion thereof may not be
reproduced or used in any manner whatsoever without the express written
permission of the publisher.

ISBN: 978-1-912155-66-8

Created by Reckless Indiscretions
Images under license from Sh

BELL & MACKENZIE
PUBLISHING LIMITED
www.bellmackenzie.com

D1440096

DRINK
GOOD BEER
WITH GOOD
FRIENDS

Life

is just a little more

honest after a

beer

The best beer in the world is the open bottle in your hand

Today I was a
hero
I rescued some
BEER
trapped in a bottle

Unlike beer LOVE doesn't
taste good when it's cold

I GOT 99 PROBLEMS & BEER SOLVES 'EM ALL!

BEER
IS LIVING
PROOF
THAT GOD LOVES US
AND WANTS US TO
BE HAPPY

Benjamin Franklin

Without beer
life would be a
mistake

Beer, if drunk in moderation, softens the temper, cheers the spirit and promotes health

Thomas Jefferson

There is no such thing as BAD BEER

it's just that some

taste better

than others

§ The best beer
is an open beer §

BEER

BEER

IT'S THE BEST DAMN DRINK IN THE WORLD

Jack Nicholson

I'VE ONLY EVER BEEN
IN LOVE
WITH A

AND A MIRROR

Sid Vicious

Reality is an
illusion
caused by a lack of
good beer

Most people hate the taste of beer to begin with. It is, however, a prejudice that many people have been able to overcome.

Winston Churchill

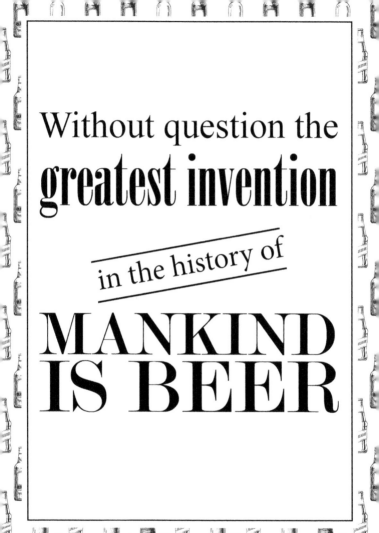

Without question the **greatest invention** in the history of **MANKIND IS BEER**

Nothing ever tasted better than a cold beer
on a beautiful afternoon

Hugh Hood

BEER
IS THE ONLY
VIRTUAL REALITY
I NEED

THE DIFFERENCE BETWEEN A
BEER
AND YOUR
OPINION
IS THAT I ASKED FOR A BEER

The problem with the *world* is that everyone is *a few beers behind*

Humphrey Bogart

Whoever drinks beer, he is quick to sleep; whoever sleeps long, does not sin; whoever does not sin, enters Heaven! Thus, let us drink beer

Martin Luther

For a quart of

ale

is a dish for a

KING

William Shakespeare

It's Saturday
The toughest decision you need
to make is Bottle or Draft

BEER

BEAUTY
LIES IN THE HANDS OF THE
BEERHOLDER

LIFE & BEER ARE
VERY SIMILAR:

CHILL

FOR BEST RESULTS

Two beer
or not two beer

William Shakesbeer

Every loaf of bread is a tragic story of grains that could have become beer

A

beergasm

is that

climatic

moment

WHEN YOU TAKE THAT FIRST SIP OF
BEER AT THE END OF THE DAY

There's more to life than beer
but not much more

BEER IS THE CAUSE OF AND THE SOLUTION TO ALL OF LIFE'S PROBLEMS

Homer Simpson

IN WINE THERE IS WISDOM
IN BEER THERE IS FREEDOM
IN WATER THERE IS BACTERIA

Benjamin Franklin

Beer

The reason I wake up every afternoon

Beer is made from hops

Hops are plants

That makes beer a type

of salad

Drinking
8 glasses
of water

seems impossible

but

8 BEERS
IS SO DAMN EASY

Step aside coffee
This is a job for beer

BEER

SAVE WATER. DRINK
BEER

I LIKE MY WATER WITH

BARLEY & HOPS

Everything important
I learned in life
I learned from

beer

History flows

forward on a

river of beer

There is more to
life
than beer alone

BUT BEER MAKES THOSE OTHER THINGS
even better

I am very picky about my
people and my beer

Shelby Lynne

I WORK UNTIL
BEER
O'CLOCK

Stephen King

BEER MAY CAUSE YOU TO

DIGRESS

AND LEAD A

HAPPIER LIFE

Michael Jackson

There cannot be good living where there is not good beer

Benjamin Franklin

A fine beer may be judged with only one sip but it's better to be thoroughly sure

I've always believed that

paradise

will have my favourite

BEER ON TAP

Irish proverb

My idea of a balanced diet is a
beer in each hand

BEER

IN DOG BEERS I'VE ONLY HAD ONE

I AM A FIRM BELIEVER IN THE

PEOPLE

IF GIVEN THE TRUTH

THEY CAN BE DEPENDED UPON TO MEET ANY

NATIONAL CRISIS

THE GREAT POINT IS TO BRING THEM

THE REAL FACTS, AND BEER

Abraham Lincoln

You can't buy happiness but you can buy beer and that's kind of the same thing

Anyone can drink beer, but it takes intelligence to enjoy beer

Stephen Beaumont

Give me a
woman

who loves beer

AND I WILL
CONQUER THE WORLD

Kaiser Wilhelm II

From man's sweat and
God's love beer came into
the world

Ed West

DRINK BEER FOR

BIG IDEAS

COFFEE

TO GET THEM DONE

GIVE A MAN A FISH

AND HE WILL HAVE FOOD FOR A DAY

TEACH HIM TO CATCH FISH

AND HE WILL SPEND ALL DAY FISHING

AND DRINKING BEER

24 hours in a day
24 beers in a case
Coincidence?

A little bit of beer is

divine medicine

Ancient Greek proverb

Beer
will change the world

I don't know how

BUT IT WILL

The mouth of a perfectly
happy man is filled with beer

BEER

Ancient Egyptian proverb

I COULD
GIVE UP BEER
BUT I'M NOT A
QUITTER

A BOTTLE OF BEER

CONTAINS MORE PHILOSOPHY THAN

ALL THE BOOKS

IN THE WORLD

Louis Pasteur

If I saved all the money

I'd spent on beer

I'd spend it on beer

Grainger Smith

A MEAL OF BREAD, CHEESE AND BEER CONSTITUTES THE PERFECT FOOD

Queen Elizabeth I